T0120725

78

Ancient Years of Grandma Elaine's Original Life Quotes with a Practical Twist for Each Day

Elaine Bolin

This book is a work of non-fiction. Unless otherwise noted, the author and the publisher make no explicit guarantees as to the accuracy of the information contained in this book and in some cases, names of people and places have been altered to protect their privacy.

WestBow Press books may be ordered through booksellers or by contacting:

WestBow Press
A Division of Thomas Nelson & Zondervan
1663 Liberty Drive
Bloomington, IN 47403
www.westbowpress.com
844-714-3454

Photo on front cover: Elaine Bolin wearing the neck tie skirt she designed and made.
Book Illustrations by Dr. Laura Koehn

ISBN: 978-1-6642-2133-8 (sc)
ISBN: 978-1-6642-2135-2 (hc)
ISBN: 978-1-6642-2134-5 (e)

Library of Congress Control Number: 2021901878

Print information available on the last page.

WestBow Press rev. date: 04/16/2021

Contents

Acknowledgements

First, I would like to express my upmost appreciation for God's gift of wisdom, encouragement, and guidance throughout my life and through this writing adventure.

And to my dear sweet family…a grateful thank you for all of the many helpful moments and things you have done for me through the writing of these quotations. First, thank you to my daughter Lorie Mills. You were a huge help in organizing, categorizing, and typing up my first thoughts. To my son Kelly Bolin. Thank you for serving as my editor. You spent hours beyond hours working closely with me through months and multiple versions and providing wisdom and guidance. You didn't try to change me—you let me be myself and helped my personality shine through. And to my husband Lendal Bolin, my son Todd Bolin, my twin brother Eldon McDaniel, and my grandchildren. Thank you for providing needed feedback throughout the process. A special thanks to Jacob Bolin for his masterful designing of the front cover and the beautiful clip art.

These are some of my original thoughts and sayings. My goal is to challenge each person with this: What good is Bible teaching if it does not have the practicality of putting it into our own lives?

-Elaine Bolin

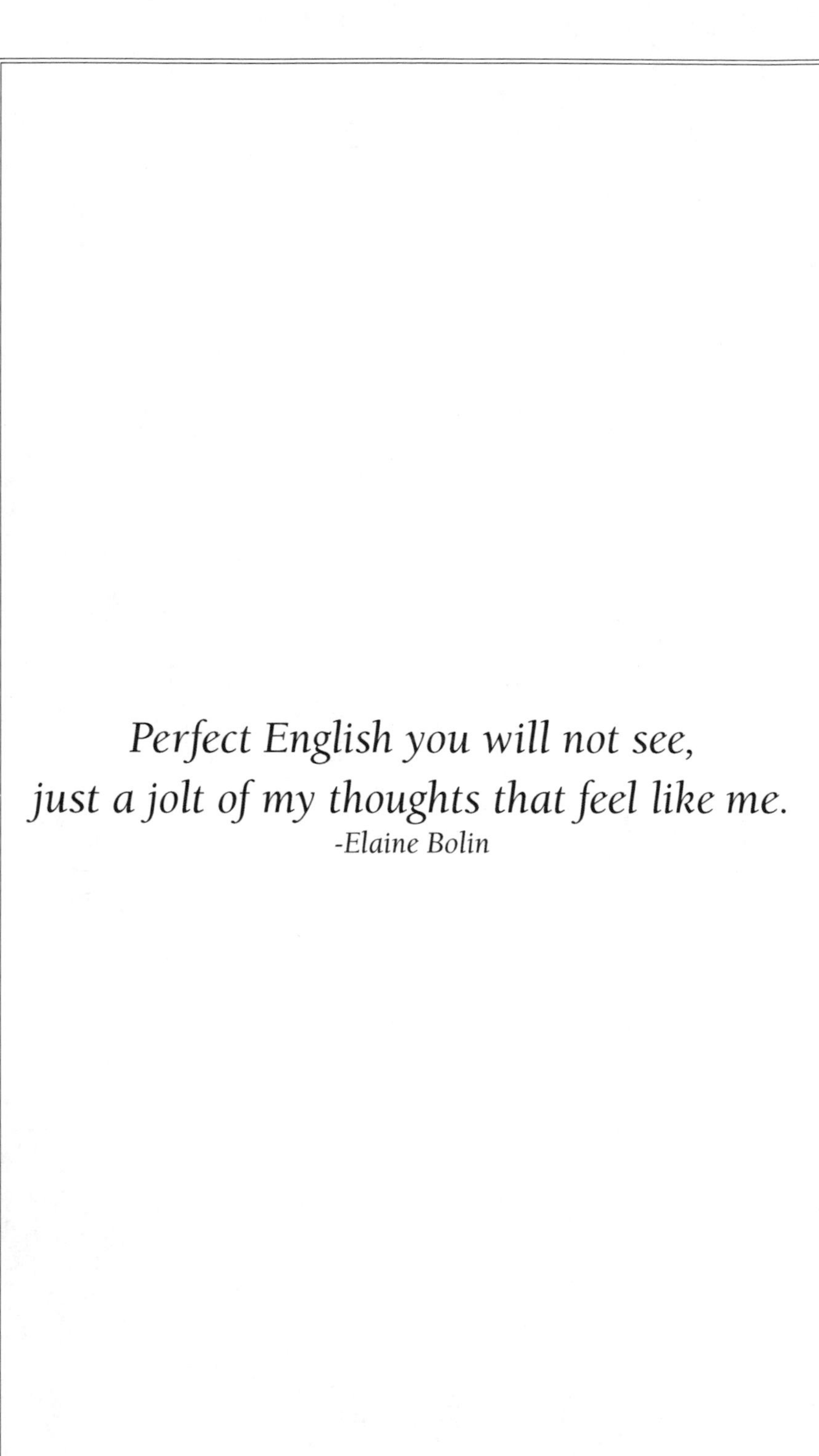

Perfect English you will not see,
just a jolt of my thoughts that feel like me.
-Elaine Bolin

Hope

Stand Up and Listen!
I hear the march of Drums
I hear drum rolls of Hope
Hope for America
Hope for the World
Hope for every person
It's Coming!
Look up and Listen

Our Spirits are lifted
Giving our Heart Hope
for the Future
we have not had

There will be answers
for your life questions
Our God will give you Hope
He will give you strength
He will give you endurance
Look up and Listen
The Drum rolls of Hope
are almost here!

-Elaine Bolin
9/11/2020

These are Grandma Elaine's thoughts with God's love left to her children, grandchildren, greats, other family members, and all cotton-patch kids!

Grandma Elaine's Thankfulness Decrees:
Always live with thankfulness to God.
All talent, all ability, all brilliance are God's Gifts!
We cannot boast. All you want to say is
"Thank you, Lord" all day long.

It takes the best in us to see the best in others.

I've always thought that it takes a lot of strength to see the best in others. But it's worth it. With God's help, seeing the best in others will anchor our life and allow us to love everyone.

Leave not the Best till last.
Give the Best till last.

Eyes smile from the heart.

Your eyes reveal what is inside of you— showing the deep feelings in your heart.

Godly Match—Public Face matches Private Face.

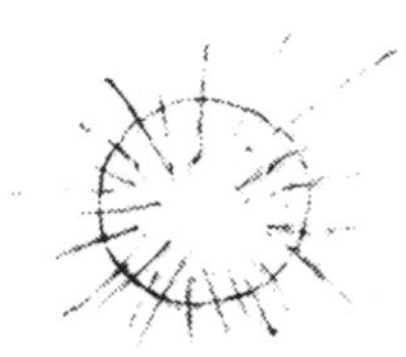

Happy am I when happy are we.

I planted a tree. Bad thoughts made it a dandelion.

I hope your good gets better.

One of my favorites that I say to everyone. I want everyone to start with the positive things already in their life rather than the negative.

I wish I knew half of what I do not know.

Reprogram your Brain: Change a negative reaction into a positive response.

You can always have a negative reaction to things that happen in your life. However, try to think hard and pray hard and let God change your mind. You can flip it and reprogram it to respond in a way that's more in line with God's plan for you.

Better to have conscious control than to have no conscience.

Yesterday's tomorrow is TODAY. Live Now.

Wait. Slow down. Be patient. This God thing works!

Have problems? Pray. Do not get in a hurry. God is in control. He will work it out for you.

Being impressed with oneself may likely leave a stupid impression.

Kindness interaction produces kindness reaction.

Healing Beams are Laughter's light.

Pure minds lead to where a Pure God lives.

Take no steps toward never.

Don't ever think never.

Here am I…So loved by God.
Here am I…So small before God.
Here am I…thankful <u>beyond</u> thankful to God.
Here am I…with no praise Great enough for our God.

Chapter 1 of life: Be.
Chapter 2 of life: Go.
Chapter 3 of life: Keep Going.

Filter your brain with God's Wisdom.
Pray. Then make the decision.

Today's Thinking is tomorrow's Action.

Everyone will be blessed if God's spirit is flowing through you.

What lies behind is what lies ahead, unless we have God's light for our pathway.

What has happened in the past will be the same thing that will happen in the future. We always say we want to change, but that is impossible unless we let God direct our path forward.

Enter into the world of Evil desires… Fall to the depth of Evil consequences.

Mark this page in your life…this is the Big Year! In fact, every year is the Big Year!

Bad Thoughts are like a brain without a Swiffer.

Little sins grow horrible weed patches in life.

Neutralize your disagreements to harmonize good memories.

Happiness is a mind-set, determined by one's self.

Happiness is something that starts and ends with your own thoughts and mind. With God's help, try to determine each morning whether you're going to be happy or not.

May the eyes of your heart be opened to see God's wisdom for you.

God always has wisdom for you, but you have to be open and listening to God for wisdom. Let Him direct you.

Make Music. Make happiness. It ain't gonna just happen. Hand in Hand with God makes Spirit-flowing music.

Satisfy the devil, he will want more.

When you accommodate the devil, he's not through with you. He will always demand more and more from you.

We are blessed in keeping our hand in the hand of our Lord through good times and bad times. Just hold on much tighter during rough times.

Who keeps me happy? God, and me.

Working with God is the only way we can be happy. And God is not going to do all the work for us.

Wisdom that is right—is God's wisdom. He loaned it to us to share with others. Ask God for this gift each day.

God has promised to give wisdom to us when we ask. And when you have God's wisdom, you need to share it with others.

He who walks alone, walks without God.

Don't give up your something for nothing.

Who shames us most? We ourselves.

Who puts the zest in our lives? The same power that made us – <u>God</u>

Integrity gives worth to life.

Integrity is the eloquence of having a good heart, having God's goodness in us. We cannot have worth in our lives if we are not integrated with God and have the goodness that's part of Him.

When we have done this "earth thing," God gently picks us up and takes us to this forever happiness made just for us.

In other words, when we die, God lovingly takes us to a forever happiness that never ends and that is made just for us.

Internal Love gives off External Love.

Kindness comes from your heart.

Conquer the worst with the Best You.

What did you think after you thought?

What did you think after you processed it? Don't draw a conclusion immediately…give it a little more thought and you might come to a different conclusion.

Calm down! God has the last word.

Negative reactions sabotage good relationships.

God gives you thoughts and ideas. Do not lose them.

Keep an open mind to the unique thoughts and ideas God wants to share with you daily.

Death frees us from the suffering we did not want…to the life we have not had.

Death frees us from this world's suffering and releases us to heaven and the life we never had. Look forward to that.

In trouble? Call on God. He has it taken care of already.

Yesterday's mistakes hold us in the grips of the past. Get loose and LIVE again!

Stand not in the lines that form to visit the past. Take not this temptation. The negative past should be forgotten.

Longing for the past is Losing the Best of your future.

Keep your days a venture forward.

Giving Up is Giving nothing.

It gives nothing to yourself. Gives nothing to God. Gives nothing to others.

Use God's Wisdom…You know why? Cause You No Wise.

We are not wise without God.

Give the better you—for the better me.

We work to be better, so we can work with each other better.

God's here. God's there. Look for Him.

If you See the worst in others, blindness would be an improvement.

Bite the bullet before it Bites you.

HOLD your TONGUE. HOLD your ACTION.

Biblical you are, when practical you be.

Unless you practice it in your own life, you are not being Biblical.

Think good thoughts. One day I thought two in one day.

Too many words make too many nothings.

Be wise with your words. Many words are not synonymous with intelligence. Listen more.

All abilities come from God. We just get to use them.

Give a field of love – Receive back a field of flowers.

Happy the days when you smile sunshine.

A smile for everyone, even strangers. A smile sends sunshine and positive energy to others. A smile shares the brightness of your life with those you meet. It helps others; it helps you too.

Prescription for failure: No need for God.

Pride makes the Best *Idiots*.

If you live yesterday twice, today gets skipped and tomorrow gets cheated.

Discouragement held: Blinds the eyes to future Surprises that God has for us.

Who Possesses heartaches is one who carries a pocket full of regrets.

The guilty run when no one's chasing.

With no guilt, you do not have to run. When you are innocent, then you have a pure conscience and don't have to be afraid.

Whoop up a little dust on your way to Everywhere.

Everyone needs to take action, try new things, be challenged, and have as much fun as possible.

Stop Not in Lonely Town – Keep on Rolling.

When you feel down and lonely, go help someone else not feel lonely.

The Day after Death: How do we adjust after loss? Take the good in our loved one and create new life in others.

What is a healthy way to process the loss of a loved one? First, we capture the good that we remember in our loved one. Then, envelop the people you see with that love. See their needs. See their good qualities. Tell them what good you see in them and encourage them to use their talents to help others. What a beautiful cycle of Life. It helps all of us. Keep the love of God moving-on through other people.

He who doesn't ever, doesn't either.

Feeling Better about me Makes Feeling better about you…Better.

When people don't feel good about themselves, they are unable to feel good about other people. Work on yourself first.

The more I sing, the better you look.

When I feel good, I see you in a better light.

Empty you feel, when kindness you don't.

Kindness fills an empty heart…yours and theirs.

Wipe the smile from your face and you will feel wiped out.

Who has life without life? Only those without God.

If you have life on earth without God, then you won't experience true life on earth, and you won't experience eternity with God.

Crawl into God's cave. Spring out with His courage.

Spending time by yourself in God's cave gives you the strength and courage for another day.

You idle? ...You boring.

Who gives – is who gets.

Evil thoughts…the saddle for Evil deeds.

Evil thoughts and evil deeds…they ride the same trail together.

Relate with love…Overlook the frailties of others.

I have frailties, you have frailties. What do we do with our frailties? Overlook them in the spirit of Love.

Stand Up, Not Out.

Do not live to be a show off.

Yesterday's Evil is today's education. Learn! Learn!

When bad things hit us, we're sad about it and often times let it hurt us. Instead, we need to let it be something that we learn from and allow it to strengthen us.

Critical are you? Then criticism you will receive.

God Is, When we are not.

God is always there for us through everything, even when we are not at our best or where we want to be. This truth gives us strength to do more.

Each Day Give God the Glory – It's already His!

Forgiving cannot be done alone. Only God's pure love can make it happen.

Well-being is well doing.

Follow me with Joy and I will follow you.

Stop the fight before the fight stops you.

God gives you a reach, higher than you.

Hold tight to God—He holds you up.

Hate warps a good mind.

Homeless are you when Heaven you lose.

The Devil does not play his cards face up.

The Devil is a manipulative master of disguise and uses shrewd and cunning tactics.

Money shared is money earned..

The Bible says if you share, it will come back to you.

God knows. We do not.

Since God knows what we do not know...Pray. He is the only one who can help us with our unknown future.

Best Exercise: Wisdom Applied.

Put God's wisdom into practice in your life.

If you want to complain, try to be original.

Hearing the same complaints over and over is tiring. Most people will turn their listening off.

Want time off? Then finish your time in.

Work hard, then Play.

Enthusiasm is contagious.

Life of Deception: Counterfeit Life.

No love. No God.

Give your best to God. Even when the best is the hardest to give.

Bring the positive to you. It won't come on its own.

Keep evil thoughts out of reach.

Appreciate All...God did it.

Let me go with Jesus into His death and burial of baptism to be raised with Him in a new, clean, changed life. My sins are forgiven. Now, I will also be God's Child forever, as Jesus is. Thank you, Lord.

Relief from emotional pain? Send it to Heaven, let God hold it for you.

Prayer is a God Privilege. He listens.

Your goal of getting money will suffocate life's priority.

Unkind words come back to bite us.

Small are we—living in God's enormous goodness.

God's law: I forgive others. God forgives me.

No matter...YOU matter.

Money is a gift from God, increasing as you share.

Today ain't gone 'till it's yesterday.

Corrupt money: Used on self only.

Honesty first—saves disgrace later.

Forget mistakes; they stunt your growth.

Genuine are you when giving
is more exciting than getting.

God forgives! So go not through life – Go not to death – without forgiving yourself and others.

Uncomfortable am I when uncomfortable are you.

Harboring mistakes muddies the water for reflective reasoning.

How do you share Goodness with your children? Get It First.

Go wherever you like, but know the Lord is watching.

You Perfect? You not a person.

Better to have my name on your heart than on the tombstone.

Lord, Do not leave me where you are not.

A stingy Person desires riches. Rich, he will never be.

Need sunshine? Put thankfulness to God in your Day.

God helps us shape the mind…
and the body follows orders.

All of Life's Production is
lost, if Heaven we receive not.

A golden treasure…giving
your best to many someone's.

Lies cheat you, sabotaging your peace.

Begrudged Gift…Worth Nothing.

Sadness are your days when kindness follows you not.

Fast Track to Heaven…Obedience.

Challenge yourself for a success you have not had.

Short cut to happiness: Read God's word and <u>listen</u>.

What language do you speak? Kindness or Cruelty?

Make the <u>best</u> of the worst. Give it a smile.

Wisdom is gone when tantalizing jealousy lingers.

Make God Your Best Friend. Talk to Him today.

Harboring evil is Paradise lost.

Give a gift in Love…or Give not.

Man of Pride…forgot His Creator.

Calm the high tide with patience.

Who combines anger with anger gets what they do not want.

What is Luxury? It's living under God's umbrella.

My Road Block...ME.

A pitfall for bad health? Pity yourself.

A grumpy grumbler is still muttering <u>nothingness</u> in his sleep.

Resentful Efforts…wasted movements.

Careless day? Ignoring loved ones.

Distrust rides with Dishonesty.

When you have one, you have the other.

Greed ruins a friendship.

Greed destroys that back and forth love of a friendship. You should want happiness for your friend. You can't have a friendship if you covet what they have.

Good habits will live Long. Carry them proudly.

Time is a gift of God…walking back to our beginning.

Time is a gift from God. We come from God in birth, and we walk back to God in death…from eternity to eternity.

Devilish deeds Cause Devilish pain.

We always pay for bad actions.

Conquer your thoughts; you Conquer your enemy.

Positive thoughts create inner peace.

Broken are we when laughter stops.

When life's a mess…start over with a new angle on your perspective.

By communicating with God and using His wisdom, create a new way to arrive at your goals.

Complicate not your life. One day's problems are enough.

God forgives to make us free to live.

He clears our life with His forgiveness, frees us, and gives us hope.

Nothing lucky in God's world.

Nothing that happens to us is luck. God is in control.

He who strikes back Strikes alone.

Let God handle the fight. God does a better job..

Get out of the way—Jesus is coming through..

*Do not get in the way of what Jesus plans
for your life. He knows best!.*

Eyes talk the truth, while lips tell the lie.

Eyes reflect the soul and are more telling.

Many words flatter your own self.

You are your only listener when you brag about yourself.

Open Heart—Open Pocket book.

Give to others graciously.

Rags to riches: trip to Heaven.

We came into the world with nothing, and we go back to God's world of luxury.

"Life is too Big for me...Take over, Lord."

Talk to Him. Make Him your first resort.

Hide not from the ghost of your past. Release it, and let it fly.

Face it and make it extinct.

God sees you before you see yourself.

God is already ahead of you and has everything worked out.

"Daddy, I'm coming—following the God that you follow."

A parent's example is so important. Children are watching their parents closely and follow in their footsteps.

Conquer your thoughts on the way to the moment.

We don't want to go into the mud twice.

Don't repeat the same mistake

Dusting cobwebs stir up the old varmints.

Jesus gives life to that dead family tree.

Itemize your frustrations. Then give them to God

A smile thinks of others

You speak to drugs…they speak back with Pain and Agony.

Death walks in with Darkness, but God carries us out with Light.

Death is a certain thing. Life is not. Heaven rescues us.

We know death is a certain part of our future. But we do not know what will happen in life. And Heaven rescues us.

He who harbors animosity keeps pain alive.

Get loose.

Sin: Too hot to hold and too hot to keep.

Walking into problems without God
is like trying to jump the Grand Canyon.

Compassion grips the heart of love—
and creates a desire to give to others.

Mended mistakes will still tote consequences.

❧

Uncomfortable am I knowing what I do not know.

❧

Seeing only…is what doing is not.

When you see a need, be the kind of person who will follow up.

❧

New ideas hide under old ideas.

**Why did I think what I thought…
when I could just not think at all.**

Do not make assumptions or think the worst. It will get you in trouble.

Save yourself misery—Take no bites of something you should not chew.

Reflective discovery…Progress we make.

Learn, Learn from the past.

Fake Life: Perished Reality.

This kind of person is not true to God or themselves

Rise up to look: God Sees what we do not See.

Pray for God's insight

A jealous heart sabotages clear and wise decisions.

Your judgment becomes twisted.

Steal not a love that's not your own.

Hold tighter to your own love.

Jesus, cover my sins. I do not want them destroying my future.

Answer me with meanness…I will answer you with God's dignity.

Only God can give us the strength to answer with His dignity and wisdom.

No Answer can be Perfect Sometimes.

God's Recipe for Life and Steady Personal Growth: Give back Love for Unkindness.

Constant dripping of Bad thoughts will corrupt your future.

Stop! Before you go to negative thoughts…Why darken your days?

Friends of the Devil make Constant Enemies.

Choosing the wrong friends will create a bond of destruction.

A little sin: escape before it takes all of You.

Evil directions start small.

Calmness makes way for thinking.

Remaining calm makes better thinking. It will allow your brain to work things out with wisdom.

Fallen into Grief? Let Jesus pick you up.

Jesus is our Best 'pick me up.

Carbon copy of you NOT MADE. Be Yourself.

Talk where you have walked.

You can't talk one way and walk another.

Grief is "a heavy"...let Jesus carry the weight.

Rubbed Wrong? Tough!

Someone upsets you? You are going to have that your whole life. Get used to it, let it go, and carry on.

May the wisdom of God be broadcast through you.

May it be spread far and wide like a radio broadcast.

My coming is running into my going.

Quick you be to mend mistakes, before mistakes unravel you.

Calm today. Calm tomorrow. A conscious habit.

You must intentionally create a mind-set of staying calm in advance of your situation. This creates a habit of wisdom.

Thankfulness is our participation with God.

A life of being thankful is what God wants from us, and this is how we participate with God. It's how we blend with God. It's pure and beautiful.

Prayer is a unity of spirits between God and us.

It is knowing that God has taken care of our needs before we get the answer. Thank you, Lord in advance for your future grace.

Give Wisdom to Hope. Then Hope Thrives.

Try to keep having hope that everything will be better. But hope cannot live on just empty hope alone. You have to apply wisdom to that hope so that it can thrive. If your reality seems like it's hopeless and you fear that you won't achieve your goals, then keep applying God's truth in your life. God will give you strength and will change you so that your hope is in something really worth hoping in. It's a hope in God alone.

Clip not your own wings in life. Jesus forgives.

If you don't allow Jesus to forgive you, you are clipping your wings and preventing yourself from soaring higher.

God lives in us as we live in His existence.

God does live in us; But the greater truth is that we live in His enormous world and He is in everything.

At the loss of a loved one: My heart will give up to memories and eternity.

When you lose a loved one, your heart has to give up everything except memories and God's utmost love for you, which will be eternity together with those that you love.

Prayer: God give us wisdom to make a life change!

What good is God's wisdom without making practical application in life.

God gives us a minute to be born, a minute to live, and a minute to die – and a forever gift with Him.

Gifts of Gladness are a contagious gift to others.

I feel that when I can share the gladness in my heart, it's a gift...and it's contagious to everyone around and helps them to look at life differently.

Sharing your best brings out the best in others.

Sharing the best in yourself (God's kindness and love) brings out the best in others.

God gave us His Spirit to find His Happiness.

Life on earth is not easy, and the devil doesn't want us to be happy. God gave us His Spirit as help so we can find happiness here on earth.

Death gives depth to the memories of life.

When someone you love dies, feelings and memories of deep beauty will link you closely to their life. Feelings of intensity about everything you knew about them and every memory has deep, deep meaning.

Wisdom turns life into a practical education.

God alone knows us best and provides perfect wisdom for how to live life. Pray for this perfect wisdom.

Tears of life can bring a wholesome future.

When you have a lot of tragedy, it can sometimes turn you around, to where you are moving in a more wholesome direction.

Hope sleeps until hope lives.

Hope sleeps until you get the reality of what you hoped for.

Since Jesus loves me, I know He loves you, and I hope my life can show you God's Love.

Pure logic can travel the road to a twisted rationalism.

Something that is true and logical can travel the road of our mind if we are not careful and be warped when we think incorrectly about things or make false assumptions.

Forgive it! Drop it! Trash it! Leave the worst in life behind. Hold on to the best of memories. This will give you peace.

Grace is a gift that cannot be repaid – only appreciated.

Pure happiness is harmony with God.

We live inside of God's absorption. He came first.

God made everything and everything came out of Him. You are living inside of the completeness of what God is and what He has made. You are living inside God's everything.

You need wisdom? Just ask God.

Ask the Source. He knows you best.

A forgiving Spirit allows growth.

Forgiving people…it's the only way you can grow. Your growth is stunted when you can't forgive someone.

Caught in the middle – Flee!

Don't get in middle of someone else's fight!

Success with Efforts, Efforts with Goals.

You can't have success without efforts, and you can't have Efforts without having Goals

Giving encouragement gives Hope—and Hope builds.

Encourage others. Encouragement changes lives. Help others to use and build on the gifts that they already have.

Jesus is the right turn.

When you're deciding what to do in your life, you can boil it down to a simple, daily decision.

Harbor the Unhappy Past... Contaminate the Future.

We waste a lot of time on bad memories. It wastes time that can be focused on the future. Pray to God and let those memories go.

Let God's Wisdom shine in Practicality.

Apply God's wisdom in practical ways.

What to do with God's wisdom? Just Obey it.

What follows us? Our children's footsteps Good or Bad. What do we leave our children? Our Example.

Clever are we when clever we are not. .

We are wisest when we realize that we don't know everything.

Take Time Out For thought and Meditation!

You keep peace…You keep health.

Make Joy the moment.

Difficulty may follow you, but a
Brave Heart comes from God.

Remember the best –Forget the rest.

Work brings challenge –
challenge brings self-rewards.

Go to others with love. Love will
come back to you in double portions.

Take with you the positive in each day.

Jesus conquered our death, gave us forever Life.

Wake up to Sunshine. Go
to bed with Sunshine.

We leave God, but God never gives up on us.

Don't let fear torment your Joy. Keep Joy close!

A Giving heart is a heart fulfilled.

Swim with Evil – Evil will take you under.

We lead together – We follow together – We Succeed together

Twisted thoughts conjure Negative momentum.

Just like Life, death is not scary; it's part of God's plan.

My Everyday Philosophy:
"Lord, Help me--I Blew it!"

This day I have. This day I use.

The magnificent GOD Created the magnificent YOU.

Food for Growth. Bible for Life Growth.

Goals are God's dream for you. God gives you a dream and He knows you can do it.

Take one step Upward. Never Back.

Savor the love you have…TIME IS SHORT.

Calm your pain with quiet meditation.

Who carries good health? The person with a happy heart.

Think Evil → do evil.

The connection between life and peace = God.

Take God out of Good – You are left with "*0*".

Destructive you be when
constructive you are not.

God's wisdom for yesterday's
planning gives tomorrow its success.

Let not the day darken before you forgive.

When Gentle thoughts evolve,
gentle is your spirit with others.

Give your good goals value…take 2 steps
toward your goal before the day is over

A life of Giving is life for the living.

Wisdom directs decisions. Decisions
direct daily adventures.

Make not the past your future.

Learn, Learn from the past.

God speaks. We listen. We learn.

Breaking down? Open your eyes to hints of a problem before it explodes into real difficulties.

Direct your decisions to direct your integrity.

Brace yourself…Life's a Wild Ride!

Winners do not ride dead horses.
Winners make wiser choices.

Valuable words become a treasure for others.

Put Calmness in your back pocket.

Jesus, don't just wash my feet – clean up my faults.

Claim the goodness, not the worstness... in every situation encountered.

Guilt: God's warning to take hold of God...so He can take hold of you.

Smart Wisdom = Wisdom shared.

Aching for a baking? then Fester a fight.

Never encourage a fight.

Search for the LOVE that is searching for you.

God is the love that is searching for you…and God has a special person for you…you just have to find them at the right time.

Distance is Closer when love is Broader.

In a relationship, be open to each other and learn to give more.

Mischief in thought…deaf and blind in heart.

If you are a good person, do not allow yourself to harbor evil thoughts or encourage thoughts of mischief towards others. If you do, you are truly deaf and blind in heart.

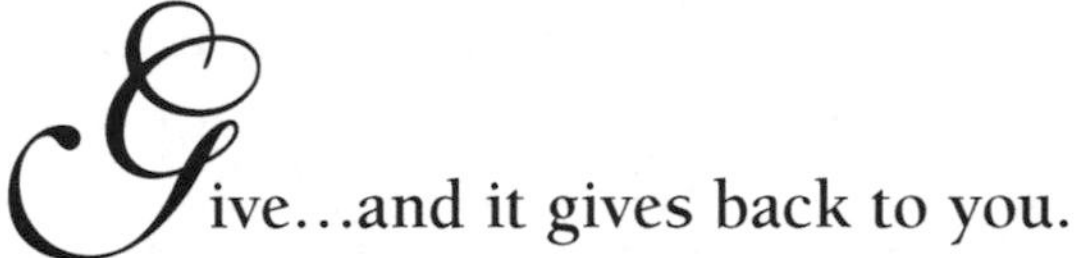

Give…and it gives back to you.

God's law in action.

Bring gladness to the madness.

Change the verbal atmosphere and usher in peace.

Lord, help us catch up with you.

We have a long way to go, but we strive to be like Jesus always.

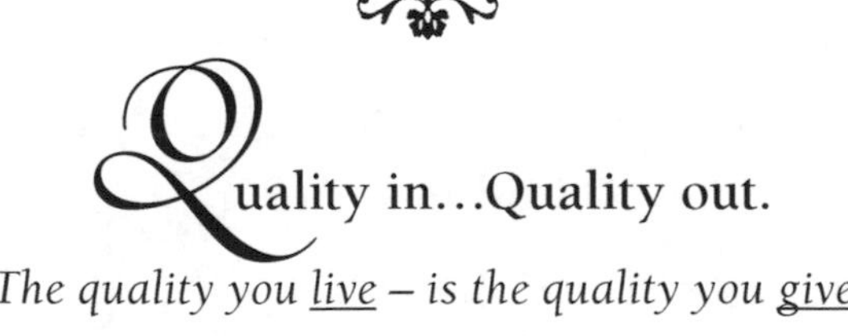

Quality in…Quality out.

The quality you live – is the quality you give.

Roll with Life's waves until you find calm waters with God.

Get comfortable with life's up and downs, knowing God will bring you to calm waters when He feels the timing is best.

Good Health…God's miracle.

We should not take good health for granted. Thankfully, every moment of good health should be considered a special blessing.

Patient are you when calmness leads.

Let calmness clear the way.

The Element of truth requires a Microscope.

Keep digging for truth—studying till you find it.

Seeing is when Saying is not.

You can see what someone did not say. Look beyond what is verbalized.

See the water boil. Enter not into it.

Do not walk into problems without talking to God first.

I see what I do not see.

I don't always see what is really there. There's often more to the story.

Conquer your Future with Your Today.

Make the best choices for your today…it will impact your future.

A healthy mind creates a healthier body.

Keep a pure mind for a healthier body.

Slippery slope when grounded we are not.

Be grounded in the Lord.

Make God's procedures our conclusions.

Make sure God is leading in our decision-making.

Hide not from reality while reality hides from you.

Hit reality 'head on.' Do not be afraid of it or avoid it. After you do that, your job is half done. The other half is to Pray!

Today's Reality is Yesterday's Hope.

Confuse not your life with yesterday's thoughts or tomorrows problems.

Thankfully, God is in control. He takes care of us, and we only waste time worrying.

Waste not your energy…give it to others.

Time given to others is God-spent.

Living under God's Umbrella,
Let Storms Come.

God is our only safety as the storms of life hover over us.

Pampering constant grief…a slow destruction of happiness.

Change your mind to the positive…a total conscious transformation of the Brain.

Get up and Plug into God, Before you run down.

Talk to God before the day begins, so you don't create your unwise mistakes, Alone.

He who carries the American Flag carries responsibility.

Take on the job of keeping America free.

Live Today before it becomes tomorrow.

Do not complicate your thoughts today.

A Heavy heart heals no one.

Let God carry your pain.

Death is a distant future coming quickly.

We think of death as being far-off in time…
but it is life that passes quickly.

Action mirrors your thoughts.

Make good thoughts mirror your good actions.

Rich you be, when family you treasure.

Saving misery pays poor dividends.

Roses for the living, not for the dying.

Send your gifts of love while people are alive. Don't wait till you have to place them on the casket.

No Barking Allowed. You're at the wrong tree.

Minimize your complaints.

Do not let the storms follow you.

Some people cause trouble wherever they go. Observe yourself closely and reflect on whether you are causing storms in your path.

Recoup…take a breath from God.

Godly living is Godly doing.

Make the *mostest* out of the *worstest.*

Can't ever is can't never.

A "can't do" mindset will never achieve anything

God-ward steps declare faster motion.

Holding the beautiful thoughts of a loved one will give you the life sparks to brighten every moment of your life always. These memories will lovingly live close to your heart every day.

Healed we be, when Laughter is Shared.

Laughter is so good for us. We need to do it more often.

You have done well. So do it again.

Up and Down, Round and Round. You, no go anywhere.

Calmness through prayer quiets the depths of the heart.

Time's not on your side. It ends when you end.

Cursing someone in the dark may be heard where there are no ears.

Take God's might to fight for right.

Riding God's current feels easy and right.

Prick the skin but do not prick the heart.

Easier to recover from pricked skin than from a wounded heart.

Wake up with the birds. They are already in action.

A tangled life torments others.

Approach madness with quiet caution.

Empty conceit falls flat.

How wonderful to feel God's
breath of love through others.

Go to others with love. Love comes back to you in double portions.

Who cares about you? I do. Who do you care about?

A listening Ear will get, in return, a listening Mind.

Foul Odor when Foul Life.

You lose what you let go.

Invest in your relationships or you'll drift apart

Picture a cheerful heart…it will develop picture perfect thoughts.

Compliment others. You will be a compliment.

Try Organized Hope.

Put your hope into action with planning and strong follow-through.

Wounded by daily distress & pain? Call on God. He retrieves us.

A mother's perfect dream… having Godly children.

-Elaine Bolin

Time

Time is a Gift of God...
Walking Back to our Beginning
to our Beginning
to our Beginning

The Way Forward...
Is not the Way Back
not the Way Back
not the Way Back

The Way Up...
Is not the Way Down
not the Way Down
not the Way Down

Yesterdays Take over Todays
Todays take over Tomorrows
Until the End of Time
the End of Time
the End of Time

Time is Yours...Until the End
Until the End
Until the End

-Elaine Bolin

Don't forget to see what fun you can have with the following section, Laughing with the Ancient Agers, which pokes a little fun at what happens as we age.

Laugh with the Ancient Agers

Good thing about being old…you do not have to do something about everything.

I lost the way by way of My Way.

Old is Comical. Till old you become.

Coming and Going Came and Went.

Top Things I say as I get older:

- Don't complicate my life with reality.
- I didn't lose my keys. My keys left me.
- These screws are on tighter than they used to be?
- I cannot keep up with me.
- You go where I cannot go.
- Here we go again—this stubborn jar will not open.
- Where did you leave what you left?

I am donating my old rusty organs
to my favorite enemy.

Playing on the X-Box...whoopeee!
It's like going fishing without the water.

New what? New hip, New
knees. Watch the body grow.

Now days, the new baseballs
are unusually difficult to throw.

Go For It. Try something New!

Oldie Goal: Beat "Harry" in a wheelchair race.

I finally trained the dog to walk…slow.

Old bodies slow down. Virtue and goodness live on.

Under the spreading chestnut tree, we sit.

Take the "cheaper" Pet Vitamins. In 2 weeks, you will be chasing cars.

Advantage in being older:
kick up, kick back, kick who?

Bury yourself not before it is time.

Carried the world on your shoulders? Time to lighten the load.

Foot Loose and Fancy free…
Now where do we go?

I found my flag, but my country's lost.

At our age, we don't have to harmonize with everyone.

Normality of the past is the unknown for the future.

You realize you are old when Friday comes the next day after Monday.

Pain does the aspirin walk. God does the miracles.

I do not remember what I did not remember.

Ears on. Eyes on. Let's roll.

I am old enough to be lazy.

Stay Young, till you get old.

Today I woke up. My brain did not.

You look as old as I feel.

No worries! Dropsy only happens when holding something.

Grandpa Mechanic back under the car and ready to go. Now, where's the car?

Don't ever get old. Just move faster.

My keeper-upper is slowing downer-downer.

End of Life disaster: Leaving nothing honorable to anyone.

Gone are the days when tomorrows are distant realities.

Up at 7 AM; Brain engaged at 10 AM.

I am not old 'till your name is "Hey You."

What did I say before I said it?

I can't remember what is funny about being old.

You are old. I am not.

We are not old, we are just gaining wisdom from our children.

Cover an old man's baldness with a Hat, but you cannot cover his wisdom.

Is your awake better than mine?

I wish I knew half of what I do not know.

Cover your white hair with
the elegance of wisdom.

I'm so old my cat kicked me back.

Hearing Aid Adjusted…
you are now tuned out.

It's so dry that Humidity has to get to 120% before it will rain.

Games Over! Who lost? Don't know, the Team is still looking for the ball.

Today's fun—a Journey to the mailbox.

Carry me back to the Past;
Just do not leave me there.

Another Birthday: a Love Gift from God.

Keep up with the Joneses. They are going Where?

We have a minute to live and a minute to die.

Life is like a vapor. It passes quickly and is gone.

Ancient are we…when Ancient we be.

Your actions are what you will be. If you don't want to feel old, change your actions.

We have to say "goodbye" so we can say "hello" again someday.

I can't imagine my "someday" without you.

New beginnings intertwine with old happenings.

Being old is a big change, but you adapt by using your past experience.

Pain grabs you. Throw it back.

But pain cannot crush your spirit. Be positive with God and let Him control your mind.

I chased the dogs down the street until they caught me.

Come what may, it's Coming!

Come back to my house, before
my house is empty.

With the radiant sunset comes the
radiant glory.

Do not leave me before I am gone.

Some days I feel like I am wearing a walker.

OOPS! I fell. Which way up?

Taking charge of my life…staying well.

Keep on your toes for
the next days surprise!

What ails me is not working right.

We meet…to meet again.

We have more cowlicks than hair?

I can't remember where I was before I was?

Current Events: Getting Up.

Came Up From Coming Down.

Enjoy Oldie jokes when you are young. They are funnier.

Back to where I was before I was.

Easier to Fall down than Fall Up.

Life everlasting – the best it gets!

Ancient age dictates constant strength.

What was I doing before
I lost what I was doing?

The great fun of being older? Exaggerating.

His breath was so bad we blocked his telephone number.

Ticks were so big they growled at us.

That Bug picked me up, threw me down. What a flu!

Complaint Department: Being Old. Getting Up. Eating.

Death is a new adventure. You have to die to Live.

Today's Excitement: Wake up the neighbors!

See me? See you? Who sees?

Open up the Book. It glares back.

Doorbell speaks softly.

Who calms the storms of your
Life? The one with the power…God.

Do not be afraid.

Death is a walk in the dark
marching toward the light.

Give me the light of God.

Turn up the sound, my brain is in the crossfire.

Sometimes thinking prevents hearing.

The Mind Works. Keep it Alive.

Do not let the mind get stagnant. Challenge it.

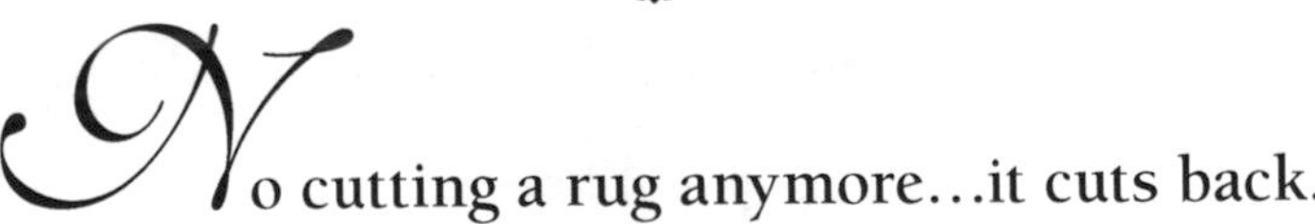

No cutting a rug anymore…it cuts back.

No quick dancing anymore. It's too painful.

Old am I when the Rooster crows all night.

Sleepless nights are like hearing an old Rooster crow all night.

The Old House shakes and rattles, holding tight to what it used to be.

Our old bodies are getting prepared for the new changes…Heaven's Beauty.

Vacancy at the grave site –
Heaven holds our future.

As you get older, you deserve
the gift of your own love. Receive it.

You have given…now it's your time to receive.

Some people have more excuses
than they have words.

So it is. So it was.

Creative we be, when spelling words are short.

Keep life simpler.

-Elaine Bolin

Discussion Guide

These thought-provoking original quotations can be useful for young people and adult discussions. Everyone will be thinking, talking, and laughing. Here is how to make a game out of your fun!

1. First person selects a quotation and reads it to the group. Then the group answers one or more of the following questions relating to the quote:
    - What do you think of when you read this quotation?
    - Tell us about your experience in a similar situation with people?
    - How would you help other people in this kind of circumstance?
    - How would you make it practical in your own life?

Then allow each person to select a quote for the group to discuss. Continue as time allows.

Meet the Author

Elaine was born in Kansas City Missouri and reared in Abilene Texas. She is a Mother of 3 grown children, 9 grand-children, and 3 great grand-children. She attended Abilene Christian University and got married when she was 18.

A studious Bible teacher and a creative energetic leader, she has overseen multiple women's and children's ministries over the years. As an example, Elaine was instrumental in starting a children's bus ministry in a small Oklahoma town. She sold enough vacuum cleaners to buy the first bus to pick up children and bring them to church. With her enthusiasm and guidance, the ministry continued to grow, and eventually added 13 more buses. At its peak, the bus program was bringing in around 400 kids every week from the small community.

Elaine started her business career in grade school, selling cards and books door to door to earn money to buy her winter coat. Later, as a young Mother, she began selling Tupperware. She became top salesman in her town, then achieved state, then national recognition in the company. Realizing she had a gift for sales, Elaine got a real estate license and quickly became top salesman in her city, very unusual for a woman at that time. She later became a Broker and then started her own real estate and property development company. In addition to real estate, Elaine started another company called *Elaine's Frills*, where she sold hand-made bridal garters, heirloom custom Santas, ladies clothing, and also marketed a line of dolls that she called the *Cotton-Patch Kids*.

Elaine says, "I'm not a writer. I started writing down my favorite sayings when my sister Louetta was diagnosed with lung cancer.

She enjoyed hearing these quotes during the rough times. The doctor gave my sister 6 months to live...God gave her 3 years!"

Elaine adds, "My goal is to challenge each person with this: What good is Bible teaching if it does not have the practicality of putting it into our own lives?"

I want to leave the best in me to the best in you!

Goodnight Hug

Cotton Patch Kids illustration above by Kelly Bolin

Goodnight to my children, grand-children, greats, extended family, and all cotton patch kids.

Between God and me, I loved sharing my thoughts. My favorite Books in the Bible are Psalms and Proverbs. Let these 2 books live in your heart with their wisdom each day. God shares the greatest wisdom with us!

I pray that God takes care of you as you take care of others.

As I temporarily say my last good-bye…may God carry your future with His Blessings. If you miss me before I part from this world, don't give it a thought...I have saved the biggest hug for you in Heaven.

Love Elaine

Printed in the United States
by Baker & Taylor Publisher Services